MW01275238

© Byron Christopher
Edmonton, Alberta

No News Release Journalism

Published April 17, 2020

Dedication & Kudos

This book is dedicated to those who searched in vain for young Tania Murrell — and to those who kept the missing child in their prayers.

Although Tania has never been found, the broad consensus is that she was abducted and murdered.

A salute to **Detective Ian Shoaf** of Edmonton Police for making it his life-long mission to find out what happened to the child.

A special thanks to friends and family of Tania — and to the family of the prime suspect, now deceased. There were some difficult interviews.

And a shout-out to reporter **Gary Poignant** of the *Edmonton Sun* for the time he invested in this story — plus a note of appreciation to his employer for the articles posted throughout this book.

A thumbs up to all media employees who worked behind the scenes: cameramen/women, technicians, writers, editors, producers ... and management. These folk never get proper credit.

Edie Power — Ms. Hawkeyes — deserves special credit for her editing skills, not just with this book but with articles posted on the Author's blog, *No News Release Journalism.*

And hugs to YOU for buying this book. It's the Author's wish to reveal key information about this case so there can be some form of closure.

If there's any good coming from this tragedy, it's that valuable lessons have been learned.

Everyone made mistakes: the perpetrator, the parents, investigators, journalists, clairvoyants — everyone it seems but young Tania Murrell.

Tania trusted adults — as children should — and she and her family paid a terrible, terrible price.

Prologue

On January 20, 1983, six-year-old Tania Murrell disappeared on her way home from an elementary school in Edmonton, Alberta, Canada.

Hundreds of searchers — police, volunteers and friends and relatives of Tania — looked high and wide for the child. But there was absolutely no trace of her. No clothing, school books ... nor phone calls. Nothing. Zip.

And no witnesses.

It's as though Tania had vanished into thin air. One moment, she's standing on a sidewalk; next moment, she's gone.

What ... happened??

The child's disappearance smells of foul play. Police believe the grade-one student was abducted and murdered.

But by whom? And why on earth would anyone do that?

A heavy-drinking acquaintance of the family would morph from a 'person of interest' to prime suspect. The man never faced criminal charges because while detectives felt they had enough evidence for a murder charge, they also felt that if it went to trial, they might not get a conviction.

This book reveals the identity of the prime suspect, and what eventually happened to him.

Chapter 1

I n the first weeks of 1983, Alberta's capital was in the grip of a deep freeze. It was so bitterly cold that car exhaust was visible, suspended in the air.

People scurried about, anxious to get to any place warm.

At around 11 in the morning on January 20th, a bundled-up Tania Murrell said goodbye to her grade-one friends and walked out of Grovenor Elementary School, in the west end of Edmonton.

The child was on her way home for lunch, and she didn't have far to go. Her home — a small, rented bungalow at 10426 - 145 Street — was only a block and a half away.

At the house, the child's aunt, Vera Stortz, was preparing a hot meal for Tania and John, Tania's younger brother.

John Murrell was in kindergarten at the same school. That morning, he got out of class expecting to see his big

sister waiting for him outside. The two would walk home together, like they always did.

But on that fateful day, sis was nowhere to be seen. It appeared as though Tania had left without her brother ... and so John walked home on his own.

The children's mother, Vivian, worked at a bakery, about a mile distant. Her husband, Jack, was a carpenter. He built new houses for Alldritt Homes on Edmonton's south side.

Some have described Jack and Vivian Murrell as party-hard folk who loved their booze, pot, rock music and Harley-Davidson motorbikes.

They were — as a family acquaintance gently put it — "everyone's-our-friend-people."

But to most, Jack and Vivian were simply two young parents whose hearts were ripped out when their child vanished, never to be seen again.

Vivian's closest friend, Heather Hansen, describes Tania as a 'very happy kid.' "Anyone would have loved to have her as a daughter," she says. "Tania was an absolute dream of a child, quiet and content. She always wanted a hug and a kiss when I left the house."

"Tania loved to dance," Hansen recalls, "... to have fun with her Barbie dolls — and play in the sandbox in the backyard."

Heather's daughter and Tania spent hours in that sandbox, laughing and talking about the strangest things, like *what are you going to be when you grow up?*

After Tania was a no-show for lunch, Vera got on the blower to Vivian at work. Right off the bat, mom didn't have a good feeling because it was unusual for her daughter not to head straight home from school.

Things just weren't adding up and Vivian began to worry. She hoped that Tania had slipped away to a friend's house — but a mother's intuition told her otherwise.

A distraught Vivian sped home. When she got there, she learned that Vera had been looking for Tania on the streets and calling out her name.

Jack also made a bee line for home. Same thing. His gut signalled something was terribly wrong ...

Chapter 2

W hen Vivian dropped around to her daughter's school, she got some dreadful news. Tania hadn't made it back to class.

Her seat remained empty.

And there was more grim news: not only had Tania's classmates not seen her, no one had.

Tania would surely be home after school, well-meaning friends assured the parents.

Vivian phoned city police and a policeman dropped by. At that stage, however, there was little the officer could do except get a picture of Tania, jot down a description of what she was wearing and start going door to door.

With the worst yet to come, Vivian and Jack were already paralyzed with fear. They didn't know what to do or where to turn.

Things became even more worrisome when Tania failed to show up at the house that evening. Where the hell was she??

Every time the back door opened, hopes were raised that Tania had made it home safely.

Vivian and Jack tried to remain positive — but there were just too many red flags. Their last, faint hope was that their daughter had spent the night at a friend's house and forgot to tell her parents.

Having an unannounced sleepover was so unlike Tania — but in the midst of the worst crisis in their lives, how the parents wished that actually happened.

Alas, there had been no sleepover ...

When Tania failed to show up for class next morning, the alarm bells really went off. There was little doubt that something terrible had happened.

For the parents, the situation was now beyond worrisome. It was gut-wrenching dreadful.

Detectives initially didn't know what to make of the child's disappearance — and neither did most reporters, myself included. I was working for *CBC Radio News* when police fired off an alert about a missing child.

At that point, it was barely a story.

Next morning, reporter Ruth Anderson was about to head out the door to cover the mysterious disappearance. I was on the assignment desk and asked Ruth to hold off until school started. She agreed.

My thinking was that it made no sense getting worked up over a youngster who may have spent the night at a friend's house.

I was wrong. Vivian was right. The mother had been telling friends she had a gut feeling something awful had happened.

The media coverage swung into high gear. The story of a missing child was leading every newscast in the city, and it would stay like that for weeks.

Both parents were now trembling and no amount of beer was going to calm their nerves.

Afraid that somebody would recognize him from the newspapers and TV, Jack shaved off his beard. Paranoia was seeping in.

Rumours were circulating that the father — a biker, though not a gang member — owed a small-time drug dealer hundreds of dollars for some marijuana he bought.

Perhaps Jack owed someone money — perhaps he didn't — but it's my belief his daughter's disappearance had nothing to do with an unpaid debt.

Vivian began second-guessing herself. She kept asking 'what if?' What if I didn't have to work that day? ... what if Vera had gone to pick the kids up from school? What if ...? What if ...? What if ...

She and her husband weren't the only ones afraid.

Everyone in the city of more than half a million was now worried — because they could relate. Parents were thinking, 'There but for the grace of God ...' while young children were terrified that a stranger was going to take them away.

Like a stone tossed into a pond, that fear radiated throughout Edmonton, the province ... and the country.

Where was Tania? Was she safe? Was she even alive? Everyone had theories, but no one really knew.

Detectives were inundated with tips ... but few turned out to be significant.

According to police, their ground search was the largest in Edmonton's history. Hundreds of city blocks were checked.

Soon after Tania vanished, so did Harley, her black dog. Foul play was not suspected; it was just one of those things. Even so, it was another hit for the family.

People hoped to hear 'breaking news' Tania had been found safe and sound and that she'd been reunited with her grateful parents.

What a joyful ending that would have been. Alas, nothing like that happened.

Chapter 3

The mysterious disappearance of a six-year-old got a lot of play in the news ... although early on, a few radio and TV stations [and newspapers] didn't get the child's name right.

Friends of the Murrells didn't recognize Tania's name when they first heard it on the news. The correct pronunciation is "tohn-ya murl."

But no big deal. What mattered is that the media did a good job of covering a very difficult story.

The city's two dailies — the *Journal* and the *Sun* — again led the way with exclusive information, thanks to good police sources perhaps ... but more often than not, the printed media [in its day, mind you] had a solid reputation for having the most complete coverage. The newspapers 'owned' the Edmonton news market.

Television and radio newsrooms, meanwhile, had a reputation for essentially doing cover versions of whatever appeared in the papers. An exception was **Ed Mason** of *CHQT,* a reporting legend who probably broke more crime stories than any radio journalist in Western Canada, if not the country.

'I think Tanya got stealed'

By GARY POIGNANT

Brandy-Jo Ewashko is afraid.

The six-year-old doesn't want to go outside alone anymore.

"I just want to stay here at home with my mommy and be safe," the worried youngster said last night.

Her best friend and classmate, Tanya Murrell, is missing. And she fears something terrible has happened to her.

"I think Tanya got stealed. Something bad happened to her," she told The Sun.

Brandy-Jo, who has had sleepless, tearful nights since her friend vanished, can't understand why someone would take Tanya away.

"That's really scary. Why would anybody want to hurt her?"

Brandy-Jo, who met Tanya two years ago in kindergarten, was supposed to go to the Murrells' home for lunch on Thursday.

But instead she ended up staying at school and ate lunch with her older brother.

"I waved goodbye to Tanya and told her we would play later after school."

"But she never came back to school."

Brandy-Jo's mother, Judy, says the disappearance has affected her daughter.

"She's been cranky and crying a lot ever since Tanya disappeared. Last night she woke me up three times to ask me if Tanya has been found yet."

And the scared six-year-old says she doesn't want to go to school anymore.

"She's afraid to go outside anymore. It really took some convincing on Friday to get her to go to school," said Judy.

Brandy-Jo hopes Tanya will be found safe.

"My mom's going to teach me to pray. I'm going to pray to God for Tanya. Maybe he can help.

"I miss her. She's very fun. We played frozen tag and house and everything together. I want her back."

Vivian Murrell once shared that reporters were using them to 'sell newspapers' — but that she and Jack were using the media as well — to help find Tania. A fair assessment, I suppose.

Tension continued to rise at the Murrell residence, the pain temporarily deadened by love and encouragement from friends and family — plus pot and beer.

But it still wasn't enough. One day Jack completely lost it, pounding his fists on the kitchen cupboard and screaming, "Why would anyone do this?"

Good question.

The wall-mounted telephone at the Murrell house rang non-stop [their number was listed in the white pages]. Most callers were helpful — offering support, tips and theories.

But not every caller had a good heart. Some took pleasure in providing false leads; one sicko even tried to extort money from the distraught family. He ended up eating prison food.

Another phoned the police tip-line to reveal that Tania's remains would be found at the bottom of a sewer drain. Police checked it out. Nada. Officers traced the call and charged the culprit with mischief.

When someone vanishes, everyone and their dog has a theory as to what went down — and why. Like a fog rolling in, rumours about 'vindictive bike gangs' began to blanket Edmonton.

Some bike gangs deal in drugs, I get that, but they don't belong to ISIS — and they don't murder kids.

TANIA'S PARENTS HURT BY RUMORS

Murrells will take lie detector to clear name: Page 3

Chapter 4

A HEARTFELT APPEAL

Several days after Tania vanished, I was looking for an entirely new angle to the story — something that hadn't been covered.

I drove around to the Murrell house, parked out front, and walked to the back where I knocked on the door.

Before anyone could answer, I was joined by *CBC TV* news reporter Warren Michaels and his cameraman. From a back alley they'd spotted me standing at the door and — uninvited — trudged through the snow to join me.

Well, I thought, so much for this interview ...

The door opened, and there stood Jack Murrell, his eyes red and puffy from crying. Jack glared at the three media strangers wanting to interview him during this most painful time. Before slamming the door in our faces, he uttered two distinct words: 'fuck off!'

I glanced at Warren, he turned my way ... and we quietly left.

And that's how I met Jack Murrell.

I returned to my car, fired up the engine and sat there for a minute or two, thinking. I then grabbed my cassette recorder and a microphone and ran to the back door.

The TV guys were no longer around.

I knocked once more. Again, Jack opened the door. "I thought I told you to fuck off!" he shouted. I shot back, "You don't tell me to fuck off ..."

Jack apologized and held the door open, all the while explaining he was down — and so pissed — because his little girl was still missing.

I told Jack I understood, as I have children of my own.

Jack hung his head and began to sob. I was touched by that.

"Maybe I can help find Tania," I offered. "How?" Jack asked, looking up. I explained that if he and his wife recorded a message to the abductor, I could put it out on the radio ... and perhaps — perhaps — whoever took Tania might hear it and set her free.

"You think that'll work?" Jack asked. I replied, "What do you have to lose, man?"

I handed Jack my Sony 142 cassette tape recorder and a microphone. It was against *CBC* policy to loan our equipment — as one radio technician dutifully pointed out — but I figured what the hell. Some rules are meant to be broken and this was one of them.

My only request of Jack was that he and Vivian speak from the heart — and not read from a prepared script. I wanted something real.

We shook hands and I turned to leave. "Oh," I said, "I'll drop by in the morning to pick up my stuff."

I returned to my car and drove home to Spruce Grove, just west of Edmonton. Supper was waiting.

Next morning, Jack was waiting at the door with my tape recorder, mike and the all-important cassette tape. I was so anxious to hear what he and Vivian had to say that I played the recording as I cut through traffic to the *CBC* building on 75th Street, about 20 minutes away.

My Lord!! Their gut-wrenching plea left me in tears ...

Here's a transcript of their message:

VIVIAN : "Hi Tania. We miss you, babe. Mom is waiting for you to come home right now. I know you want to come home ... and who's got ya, you gotta tell him that you want to come home. Just tell him he knows you're a good girl and you gotta come home."

"We gotta do ballet ..."

"And John wants you home ..."

"Mom doesn't know what to do anymore; she misses you so much. But whoever has you, just drop her off at some place warm. We don't want to see who you are, just bring my baby home ..."

"She does want to come home. She loves her Mom. She loves her Dad, her kittens, her 'puppers.' And she's gotta come home. She wants to come home. You know she wants to come home. Please make Tania come home ..."

JACK : "Whoever you are, if you got my Tania [sigh] and you're keeping her warm and safe, that means you must care about her. If you care about her, let her come home."

"Please. Please, just let our little girl come home ... just take her someplace where somebody can find her." [sigh]

VIVIAN : "Okay, this is to whoever ... if you need money, we don't have any money but we can get money for you. If you need that, you just phone us and we'll help you out, borrow money. It doesn't even matter, we gotta bring Tania home. We'll get you some money if you want money."

"We got a lot of friends that love Tania."

"We really miss her. We've been trying so hard to find her and we just don't want her out in the cold. We just can't have that little girl out in the cold anywhere."

"We have to have Tania back because we just have to ... and we need her more than you need her. And I know she wants to come home ..."

[End of plea]

Peter Hutchinson, producer of *Edmonton-AM, CBC Radio's* current affairs program, teared up when the tape was played in our on-air studio.

The voices of a grief-stricken couple begging for the safe return of their young daughter not only stunned veteran journalists like Hutchinson, it shook everyone who had their radios tuned to *Edmonton AM*. The parents' painful message was the talk of the town.

A day or so later, Vivian and Jack Murrell followed it up with a news conference in their small living room where they essentially made the same plea — this time before half a dozen reporters and television cameras.

The Author in the CBC Radio newsroom; late 1980s. On the desk is the tape recorder Vivian and Jack used.

Chapter 5

A MASSIVE SEARCH ... AND A SURPRISE REWARD

Little Tania was now on the minds of many, not just in Edmonton but across Canada and the United States. Her story would be featured on the American TV program, *Unsolved Mysteries*.

In Edmonton, searchers plastered Tania posters on utility poles, bus shelters, at truck stops and in shopping malls — in the hope that someone, somewhere, knew something.

HEIGHT: **3 Feet 6 Inches**

WEIGHT: **45 Pounds**

HAIR: **Blond**

EYES: **Brown**

LAST SEEN WEARING:

Blue Coat With White Fur Collar

Green Corduroy Knickers

Black Harley-Davidson T-Shirt

Brown Boots

Volunteers searched day and night for the child. They combed backyards, ravines, abandoned vehicles — and garbage cans. This went on for weeks.

I was with a group of searchers one night when garbage cans were being checked. Lifting plastic grocery bags and assessing their weight made some wonder if they were holding human body parts.

It was still bitterly cold and the consensus was that if Tania had been murdered, it would have been almost impossible to bury her body in the ground. She had to be hidden somewhere.

Peter Pocklington, owner of the Edmonton Oilers of the National Hockey League, quietly offered a 25-thousand dollar reward for information leading to Tania's return. I say *quietly* because there was no fanfare.

The businessman also provided Jack and Vivian with tickets to an Oiler game. When the game ended, the couple headed off to the dressing room to meet the players. Jack said he didn't recognize the name of every Oiler who shook his hand — but I suspect there wasn't one player who didn't know about his daughter.

Tania Murrell had become one of the best-known children in the country, and for all the wrong reasons.

Chapter 6

NO HAPPY MEDIUM

Not long after Tania vanished, the *Edmonton Sun* published an article about a psychic who claimed Tania had been scooped by a bearded man. For a few days, every man in the city sporting a beard got second looks.

That story alone demonstrated the power and influence of the news media.

Vivian Murrell dealt with more than half a dozen mediums, desperately hoping to find out what happened to her daughter. Not one wanted to be paid.

The mother once remarked that she felt at peace after a phone chat she had with a female psychic in Calgary, pointing out it was the first time in weeks that she didn't need medication to fall sleep. She'd been popping sleeping pills.

Vivian also shared a 'finding' from another female psychic, this one in the U.S.: *the man who grabbed her daughter had driven by the house before he went to the school.* If that was true, the abductor not only knew where Tania lived — but probably knew her parents as well.

And if *that* was accurate, it would have made perfect sense for the perpetrator to first scoot by the house — to make sure Jack's vehicle wasn't parked there. He would have been in big trouble had he taken off with Tania ... with biker dad looking on.

I queried a family friend if Jack would have assaulted an abductor. "Assaulted?" she asked in disbelief. "Jack would've beat the fucker to death."

Another medium Vivian had dealings with was a former RCMP officer who flew in from British Columbia. I spent some time with him and paid attention to what he had to say.

It was my first experience with a clairvoyant. I tried to keep an open mind about his 'readings' but frankly, I didn't know what to believe.

The retired cop identified a large house nearby he claimed was somehow connected to Tania, and he gave a precise location ... just off Groat Road. Could this be where the child was being held?

I checked it out and, yes, Tania had been at the house — a good number of times. Turns out, it was the home of one of her school friends and she'd gone there to play.

That was fascinating stuff, but weird too. The man did that reading from his home in Kelowna.

The psychic and I didn't always get along. He criticized me for being impatient, saying the information I was so anxious to get would come in its own time, adding that I had much to learn about the spirit world.

He then made another claim — that human blood would be found in the basement of a house not too far from where the Murrells were living.

He described the one-storey house as having a steep arch over the front door, similar to a lancet design. Off I went to find the mystery house ...

I located a deserted dwelling that matched the description [it was the only one like it in the area]. I passed the address on to Jack.

Well. Jack broke into the house and — what do you know? — he came across a bloody mess on the concrete floor in the basement.

False alarm. According to police, a former tenant cut himself with a circular saw and neglected to clean up the mess.

Officers made allowances for Jack breaking the law —
said they understood his desperation — but warned him
that he shouldn't be doing stuff like that.

Before Tania vanished, Vivian and Jack had plans to
move to a larger house, about a mile away. They eventually did — to another rental, at 9913 - 151 Street.

One night I was with the ex-cop-turned-psychic at
the new residence. He was there to pick up some of
Tania's clothing — plus keys to Murrell's previous home,
the one on 145 Street.

And that's where we headed ...

We unlocked the front door and, flicking on a hall
light, walked in. Our voices and footsteps echoed
throughout the empty rooms.

It was a real downer walking into the kids' bedroom.
How Vivian and Jack must have cried when they packed
up Tania's clothes and toys. I can't tell you how sad I felt
standing there trying to get my head around that.

We continued our tour of the empty house. The
psychic then asked if I would check a small trap door for
the attic. He wanted to know if it was sealed. It was —
thanks to layers of paint. It hadn't been opened in years.

"That's not good," he offered, as I landed on the floor with a thud. "Police," he said, "should have looked in the attic." He pointed out that immediate family members are always suspects in cases like this.

Our final stop was the basement. We hit a light switch at the top of a flight of wooden stairs ... but nothing happened. The light was burnt out. Not to worry. We had a flashlight.

We slowly made our way into the basement, mindful of every step because there was no railing on the narrow stairs.

We were soon in for a big surprise ...

While Mr. Psychic was shining his light above the wooden beams, I wandered off towards a large room in the darkened southeast corner.

The room had a door and the door was open, but I didn't walk in. I stood with my back to the door watching the flashlight beam flit here and there.

Without warning from inside the room, a man's voice bellowed, "Who's there?!" Christ! I nearly pissed myself. Thump, thump went the old ticker.

Vivian forgot to tell us that a boarder still lived in the basement. Thank you, Mrs. Murrell for the near heart attack.

I was shaking in my boots but the ex-cop wasn't. Mr. Cool calmly walked over, shining his light inside the room to reveal a man in his 20s in bed, with the covers pulled up to his face. He squinted and gave us his name and shared that he was a worker at a meat packing plant on the other side of town.

The man answered our questions — but he also had one of his own. He wanted to know if there was any update with Tania. Nothing new, we told him.

Before we bid the gentleman good night and made our way up the stairs, we apologized for scaring the living daylights out of him.

Edmonton Police hadn't checked the attic, but they did check out the boarder. The man's alibi was solid; he'd been at work when Tania vanished.

The Murrells would have dealings with yet another medium — one who provided information that would turn the case on its head.

His name was **Ralph Hurst.** You'll get to know him in Chapter 9.

What did police think of these clairvoyants? The impression I got — at least from this case — was that they looked at all evidence, no matter the source.

However, police seemed reluctant to admit publicly they used mediums, or to give credibility to what they had to say.

Chapter 7

THE SPOTLIGHT FADES

Time moved on. The long days turned into long weeks and the weeks into months. It was a sad spring, a sad summer, a sad Thanksgiving and a really sad Christmas.

Vivian and Jack put up Tania's Christmas stocking hoping she'd come marching through the door.

Tania Murrell was also no longer a lead story. She wasn't a story at all, save for when Vivian gave a talk about missing children or when the pair commented on the anniversary of the tragedy.

It was now obvious that Tania had been abducted. There was no other explanation. The only questions people had: Was she alive? And where was she?

It was a warm spring day when I dropped by the Murrell house. I happened to be in the neighbourhood and had a few minutes to spare. Besides, we never know when a nugget will land in our lap ...

It wasn't long before Vivian dropped the small talk about the weather and her flowers and got talking about her missing daughter. She'd come to the realization that Tania had been taken — but by whom — she didn't know. Not a clue.

She never once mentioned the name of any suspect, but she did reveal that within a mile's radius of their home lived a dozen or more sexual deviants. She said police told her that. "Who would have thought?" she added.

Vivian was hoping that whoever had Tania was very wealthy and "spoiling her rotten." That struck me as ridiculous but if the fantasy gave Vivian some solace, I was good with it.

I said not a word.

Hope was keeping the mother alive — and somewhat sane.

Another time, Vivian and I were chatting in her living room when the phone rang. She pulled away to answer it, indicating it was a call she was expecting and that she'd be a few minutes.

That left me standing there, and I spotted a photo album on a bookcase ...

I began flipping the pages, looking for snapshots of Tania. Whoa! Here was something I didn't expect to see in a family photo album: party pictures ...

It must have been extremely warm when those pictures were taken — either that, or people had too much to drink — because some women were exposing themselves. I thought, this ain't right; kids could see this stuff.

When Vivian got off the phone, I asked, "What's with this?" She walked over to see what had grabbed my attention. "Oh," she said, trying to downplay things, "those are just party pictures ..."

The point I was making is that why would anyone have stuff like that in a family photo album — on display in a living room, of all places? Shouldn't they be in a box hidden somewhere in the basement?

If I had been lucky enough to have been at those parties, that's where I'd have my pictures.

There are no perfect mothers and fathers, I get that. Raising children isn't easy and all parents struggle to be good moms and dads. Been there. Done that. However, for Jack and Vivian — both high school dropouts — parenting was even more challenging because of excessive drinking, cigarettes and dope.

Here's where this is going: A dysfunctional family situation made the Murrells vulnerable to party-hard outsiders.

One such individual — a deviant and a manipulator — was accepted unconditionally into the Murrell family.

Huge mistake.

Could it be that in spite of Jack and Vivian possessing PhD's in Street Smarts, they were easy prey?

Chapter 8

I n 1984, Vivian Murrell organized Canada's first agency to help find missing kids. The idea was to create awareness and "to bring the children home."

She founded the non-profit Tania Murrell Missing Children Society.

The organization accepted donations to help cover expenses. No one drew a salary; any work was done by volunteers.

Vivian was quite excited about what she had set up. I recall the pure joy in her voice when she called to share how she had formed her own charity. She talked 100 words a minute with gusts to 150.

In that respect, her Society was therapeutic. Vivian threw herself into organizing public events and when she gave talks, she spoke with passion.

Vivian's spirits had been lifted and for the very first time, I got a glimpse of what she must've been like before January 20, 1983.

Tania's abduction had sucked the life out of Vivian, but the charity brought some of it back. I could see that she was improving. She had more spark and she didn't cry as much.

However, The Tania Murrell Missing Children Society was around for only a few years. In May 1987, Vivian handed everything over to the Missing Children Society of Canada, based in Calgary.

Murrell said she also gave them her manuscript on Tania ... but it disappeared somehow. I phoned the Missing Children Society about this and they promised to call back. That about ten years ago; haven't heard a peep.

The Tania Murrell Missing Children Society
9913 - 151 Street
Edmonton, Alberta.
T5P 1T2.
January 27, 1984.

Telephone: (403) 456-0874

Dear ____,

There are many people who are shocked by the problem of Missing Children; many who are horrified, but just shake their heads and turn away.

The Tania Murrell Missing Children Society thanks you for not turning away from this problem. Thank you for caring enough to take action and become a member of our Society. Even if you wish to be a non-active member, your support is ever needed and we welcome you to our group.

The Tania Murrell Missing Children Society has a long road ahead and everyday we are learning more about the tragic, epidemic problem of Missing Children. With your continued support we will be able to study the problem, analyze it and understand the reason it plagues our Nation. Through understanding love and determination we hope to aid the families and children afflicted and ultimately stop child abduction.

We will be in contact with you further upon our progress and you will be notified if a program of the Society is active in your area. We would appreciate your further assistance at that time.

Most important, at this time we hope you will spread the word of the Society and make people aware of our existence as much as the problem we face.

Again, we thank you for helping us begin our work to bring the children home.

Yours sincerely,

Vivian Murrell, Director

P.S. You, as a member, have an open invitation to attend any members meeting of The Tania Murrell Missing Children Society. For information re meetings, programs or involvement, please do not hesitate to contact us. Your suggestions are welcome and we look forward to meeting you.

Chapter 9

CLAIRVOYANT RALPH HURST

It was at a news conference in 1984 at the posh Westin Hotel in downtown Edmonton, where I met a clairvoyant who would turn the Tania case on its head.

The 'newser' had been arranged by organizers of a Psychic Fair, an annual event in the city. Hurst was one of half a dozen mediums from Western Canada who sat behind a long table in a conference room.

There was an equal number of reporters, myself included. We peppered the psychics with questions, then broke up for one-on-one interviews.

I chose a soft-soften man with a British accent, Ralph Hurst of Clearbrook, British Columbia.

Hurst was a nervous sort, but that may have been because of a comment I made about his line of work having its share of fakes. The man agreed — but insisted he was not a fake.

Looking to make a recovery, I asked, "Is it true that 'spirit guardians' look after us?" "Yes," the Brit responded.

Hurst continued, "I can see your guardian, just above your left shoulder. He's Chinese." "May I ask him something?" I asked ... "in Chinese?"

Hurst didn't bat an eye. "Go ahead," he said. And so I fired off my question in Mandarin: 你是如何在中国. Hope I spelled that right.

The medium confidently responded, "He says his health is fine. What did you ask him?" I replied, "I asked how he was ..."

BANG.

Without missing a beat, Hurst shot back, "Do you have any more questions?" Gotta admit, that handcuffed me. Far as I could tell, Hurst didn't speak Mandarin. [I don't by the way ... just a phrase or two.]

The man now had my undivided attention. The subject changed ... to Hurst's childhood in England. He played in his bedroom, he said, with children from the spirit world. And just as his parents were amazed that their son could see 'dead people,' the lad was equally amazed others couldn't see them.

Mr. Clairvoyant shared that dealing with the spirit world was like looking out a window at night ... he could make out outlines, but they weren't always clear.

I changed the topic to Tania Murrell, though I didn't mention her by name. I asked Hurst if he could come up with information on a six-year-old Edmonton girl missing since January 1983.

"Does her name begin with 'T'? he asked. "Correct ... you heard about her on the news?" "No," he replied, " ... I picked that up from you ..."

Hurst then said something which made me question his psychic abilities. He claimed the Murrells had two other children [as opposed to one].

I shook my head. "That isn't right," I said, "there's only one other child, a boy."

But Hurst stood firm. "Sorry," he said, "I'm picking up there's a second child ..."

I pointed out that I knew the family well ... and with him claiming there was another child just proved my point that psychics sometimes blow it. However, Hurst stuck to his guns, adding that the second child was living with the family.

Now things were getting ridiculous.

In spite of our differences, we parted on friendly terms.

A few days later, I phoned Vivian to tell her about my encounter with the psychic. I barely got beyond 'hello' when she exclaimed, "Byron, I'm going to have a baby!"

Whoa!

I immediately rang Ralph Hurst in British Columbia. He was in hospital, his wife explained, suffering from exhaustion. I left an apology to pass on to her husband ... and my best wishes for his speedy recovery.

Hurst eventually called back. "Forget it," he said, "No need to apologize ..."

Well that was classy.

Vivian's third chid, Elysia, was born on November 12, 1984.

Hurst mailed a cassette with his 'reading' on the Tania case. Unfortunately, it contained little useful information — except he felt that Jack was in a 'sticky financial situation' and somebody wasn't happy with him, adding however he didn't think it had anything to do with Tania's disappearance.

In a second reading, Hurst claimed the suspect had killed another child — a boy whose name started with 'K.' He thought it might be Kevin, but wasn't sure.

The clairvoyant said Tania was not a 'silly girl' and that she wasn't prone to going off with strangers.

He nailed that one. Vivian had trained her daughter not to speak to strangers. Out on the sidewalk, the mother banged on pots and pans, telling her daughter, "I'm a stranger! I'm a stranger! Run into the house!"

Stop right there. How many parents — especially in that era — would have gone to that length to street-proof their children? I couldn't help wonder if Vivian Murrell had a premonition that someone, some day, would take Tania ...

The story was corroborated by Brenda Dawson, Tania's babysitter.

She recalled driving near the Murrell house when it was raining heavily. Tania and John were on the sidewalk, on their way home — and getting soaked. Brenda rolled down her window and offered to give the youngsters a lift — but they refused to get in. And mind you, she was their babysitter.

Let's jump ahead to January 20, 1983. The fact that Tania got into a vehicle— without making any fuss — indicates she knew the person well.

The list of possible suspects suddenly became very manageable.

When Ralph Hurst came back to Edmonton for another psychic fair, we connected again.

This time we shared a meal at Boston Pizza. And of course, we got talking about Tania. "I have something to show you," I said, and I handed Ralph a poem hand-written on a single sheet of paper.

Hurst didn't read it right away. He turned the page over and closed his eyes ...

"Oh," he shuddered, "whoever wrote this has great remorse. It's a man ... and he's crying. He keeps saying, 'I'm sorry, I'm sorry, I'm sorry' ..."

Hurst then read the poem and handed it back without commenting on it. The actual poem and a transcription appear in Chapter 10.

I asked Mr. Clairvoyant if he had any insight how Tania died. His answer: He could feel squeezing on his throat [and some pain], plus pressure at the back of his neck. Strangulation.

Hurst felt that Tania's body had not been dismembered and that she was fully clothed when she was buried.

According to Hurst, her remains were initially stored in a cool area — such as a freezer — where they remained for weeks.

He says the child's fate was sealed after she told the abductor she'd tell her dad about something they'd done. Hurst did not elaborate.

The medium and I then left the restaurant and headed to the west end. It was a quiet, peaceful evening, around 7:30 or so, when we pulled up in front of Tania's school.

Hurst asked that I not interrupt him as he 'went back' to the morning of January 20, 1983 ...

There's a set of main doors at Grovenor Elementary School where staff and children come and go. It was my understanding that Tania had left through these doors. But according to Hurst, she left through doors at the south end of the building. That was news to me.

Edmonton Police say Hurst was correct.

Hurst 'saw' what he described as a lot of smoke at the rear of the sedan that spirited Tania away. Correct. Sort of. Because of the extremely cold temperatures, vehicles in Edmonton that day emitted exhaust fumes that froze in the air.

Hurst's account is that the passenger door swung open and Tania willingly got in. No fuss.

He also says the driver was checking out two other children on the sidewalk, same side. They'd left school at the same time and were about 60 feet ahead of Tania, walking north. However, the children didn't look behind them. Again, news to me. Were there in fact two other children on the same sidewalk, just ahead of Tania?

Yes.

Mr. Medium says the driver was 'shit-faced' [drunk or under the influence of drugs] — and that he'd driven around the school a number of times looking for Tania. He also said the man had gone by her house before heading to the school.

Hurst was the second medium to make that claim.

I told Hurst that I'd show him the Murrell house, one street over. "No, I'll show you the house," he countered.

It didn't take him long to pick out Tania's home. Of the two dozen houses on the street, the man nailed it. "That's it!" he exclaimed, pointing to a small white bungalow on the west side. I stopped the car but Hurst asked that I drive forward a tad ...

"At the back, on the right," he said, leaning and pointing, "... that was Tania's bedroom."

Correct again. Hurst was now knocking them out of the park.

"Wow!" I said, "that's crazy! How the hell do you do that?"

Hurst further claimed that Tania's body was stuffed in three plastic garbage bags and buried two feet down in what he described as a 'soggy area.' He provided three signs where that would be: a broken-down fence, a large letter 'A' and a small body of water.

That wasn't a lot to go on. I pulled out a map of Edmonton showing the North Saskatchewan River and some man-made lakes. But Hurst said the body of water he 'saw' wasn't like anything on my map.

Hmmm. Interesting ... but not very useful.

We then drove about a mile south of Tania's house ... onto Summit Drive, a quiet street in an older but well-kept residential area. The road snakes along the southern edge of MacKinnon Ravine Park.

As we approached 143 Street, Hurst shouted, "STOP! There's the broken fence!" So I pulled over. To our left was a fallen fence rail. Sign #1.

Hurst was pumped.

We climbed down into the ravine at the 142 Street overpass, a four-lane structure supported by a number of massive, round concrete pillars.

At the very top of the pillar at the southwest corner was a spray-painted, large letter 'A.' It was more than three feet tall with a big circle around it. How the heck anyone got up there to paint that is beyond me. But who cares. Sign #2.

Around the base of the pillar was a wide depression, perhaps 20 feet across, and it was filled with run-off water. "There's the body of water!" announced Hurst. Sign #3.

I too was worked up, gotta admit. But my excitement quickly diminished when Hurst shared he wasn't very good at finding dead bodies.

The ravine was steep and heavily-treed, and I had no idea where to start looking. In the summer of 2012, I returned with a shovel and metal detector, hoping to pick up signals from a buried coat zipper, buttons or metal clasps on the child's winter boots.

On one outing, I was given a hand by two private detectives from Calgary, Bruce Dunne and Shelly Nowell. Thank you, Bruce and Shelly. Sorry about the mosquitos.

I returned to the ravine several more times, once with J.T. Lemiski, a reporter with *CFCW Radio*.

We unearthed buried cans, nails, an ax head and a rusted bicycle — but no small human skeleton wrapped in rotting garbage bags.

Plus, I cut my forearm when I took a tumble and slammed into a tree. Nothing serious; band-aid time.

We scanned perhaps 10 to 15 percent of the area.

Is Tania's body buried somewhere in that ravine? It's hard to say.

Everyone has an opinion where the child's body might be. Another psychic [this one in Calgary] maintains the remains are not in that ravine, but couldn't say where they are. Here we go again.

Edmonton Police detective Ian Shoaf felt that Tania's body could be buried in Strathcona County, just east of Edmonton. That's because the prime suspect had worked there and he knew the area. That makes sense.

Given that Tania's body was never found, Shoaf felt it was another indication that Tania was not killed by a stranger. A stranger, he said, would not have had feelings for his victim and he or she would've just dumped the body somewhere.

Seeing how Tania reacted to strangers, it's fair to assume that whoever drove off with her had the child's trust.

Chapter 10

IMPACT

I t would be impossible to list all those who were impacted by what happened to Tania. There are just so, so many ...

In this chapter, I will focus on two individuals. One was at the epicentre of the tragedy; the other lived close by.

We hear a lot about how bikers are a tough lot. Jack Murrell was a biker. When his daughter suddenly vanished — never to be seen or held again — it demonstrated how vulnerable humans really are, no matter how they like to present themselves.

I sometimes wonder if these "tough" guys aren't really masking their own demons by hiding behind tough talk, threats of violence and anti-social behaviour. Pardon me for playing shrink.

I once had a chance meeting with Jack in Spruce Grove. It was a warm summer evening and I was at some event, forgot now what it was, and I was told that Jack Murrell was there. So I went looking for him.

I found Jack outside in the parking lot. He was alone and he was crying. I approached and asked, "What's wrong?"

Jack swore — and said he'd like to see one of my girls abducted, then I'd know how it felt ...

Wow! Never in 100 years did I expect to hear something like that.

In that respect, Jack was very different than Vivian. Vivian often cried — always apologizing for the way she looked, as if that was important — but she never lashed out.

To be fair, Jack was Tania's dad and he loved his daughter very much. The man must have cried a million tears after Tania was taken. The abduction amounted to a death sentence for him.

Celine Stevenson met John Murrell when she started elementary school.

"A sturdy looking boy with shaggy, blond hair," Celine recalls of the six-year old. "A slight lisp to his husky voice — and the saddest eyes."

"On John's very first day of grade one, our teacher made him stand in front of the class and basically had him showcase his claim to fame as the brother of a kidnapped child. It was awful."

Turns out, the Stevensons and Murrells lived close by. As children, Celine and John would spend time in each other's home.

"John's parents were very kind," she says, "[they tried] to maintain a positive and a happy home atmosphere. However, I was aware of their sadness and I could see their daughter's disappearance had broken them."

"They always made me promise to phone the second I arrived home. And most times," Celine adds, "John would insist on walking me there himself."

"The following year, the Murrells moved away and I never saw them again."

Chapter 11

THE PRIME SUSPECT

The two questions asked most often about Tania: 1] where is she? — 2] and who took her?

I spent a lot of time thinking about what happened to the child and I can only imagine what police officers — especially detectives on the file — pondered as they tried to connect the dots.

Suspects ranged from local perverts, ripped-off drug dealers, millionaires in the Middle East — and Lorne Thomas.

The bizarre behaviour of Thomas — the Murrells' drinking buddy — the one who often slept over — got the attention of city police.

When detectives learned that Thomas had written a poem — believed to be about Tania — his stock as prime suspect went through the roof.

Lorne Thomas died from cancer in Ontario on August 10, 2016. He took his final breath at his home in the village of Courtright, south of Sarnia.

Thomas is staunchly defended by his family. They believe it's ludicrous that police — reporters — anyone — would think Lorne abducted and killed Tania Murrell.

As for the suspect wearing a baseball cap and sporting a beard — as some psychics believe — the world is full of bearded men who wear baseball caps. That doesn't carry much weight.

And ditto ... the fact that Thomas drank a lot and smoked pot. So what.

However, what should be noted is what Thomas did while he was hammered — such as the time he and Jack Murrell were drinking beer and Jack fell asleep on the couch. He awoke to find Lorne trying to get in at his zipper ...

What's even more puzzling is after that bizarro moment, Jack and Vivian allowed 'Uncle Lorne' to take their children camping. Like that makes sense.

Vivian's response was that Lorne was drunk when he tried to open Jack's fly, so no big deal.

When I went around to the house, just a few days after Tania was abducted, Thomas blocked me from entering the kitchen, poking his finger in my chest and announcing to everyone that I was not a reporter but a 'fucking cop.'

It didn't help that I had a Russian winter hat similar to what the Mounties wear.

Vivian intervened and I got in and worked the crowd. I learned that it was Lorne Thomas who was screening phone calls [tips] made to the Murrell house.

Within an hour, Thomas and I were walking together in the cold night, lifting lids off garbage cans. I was looking for Tania's frozen body — or parts of it.

Thomas seemed strangely disinterested in what I was doing and for someone who was close to the Murrells, that struck me as odd. I peered into the garbage cans while Lorne checked out the star-filled sky. He seemed to be in another world.

At that stage, I didn't suspect Lorne Thomas. He stuck me as a man who sought solace in the bottle ... and hung out with people who liked their booze as much as he did. There was nothing terribly unusual about that.

Brenda Dawson, Tania's babysitter, gave me some bombshell evidence — a poem Thomas had penned right after Tania vanished. He wanted her to type it out so he could enter it in a contest. [It was never typed.]

Could Never Be.

Tho the day be far away, or the night just closing in
Remembering the fun they had that day and feelings possessed within.
Gazing into the distant stars, the plans they made, so bright and new
As they walked along that deserted beach, all their problems were so few
The time alone, just themselves, warm new feelings, so tender and strange
Nervous thoughts of love, of making love, passionately, their lives would change
Undisturbed, but for the waves, closely embraced, on the beach they lay
The summer ended much too soon and for them, their final day!
Precious new feelings that they shared, knowing soon, would have to end.
The tears flowed with their final kiss, it was their first love, they couldn't pretend
Often they wished, to turn back time, oh, for time to have stood still!
Bye, to turn back time, but time goes on, it's nature's will.
To return some day, they said they would, but I knew — we never could

I'm not sure what to make of this. Was it about Tania?

'Could Never Be'

Tho the day be far away, or the night just closing in
Remembering the fun that they had that day and feelings possessed within.

Gazing into the distant stars, the plans they made, so
bright and new

As they walked along that deserted beach, all their
problems, were so few

The time alone, just themselves, warm new feelings, so
tender and strange

Nervous thoughts of love, of making love, passionately, their lives would change

Undisturbed, but for the waves, closely embraced, on
the beach they lay

The summer ended much too soon and for them, their
final day!

Precious new feelings that they shared, knowing soon,
would have to end.

The tears flowed with their final kiss, it was their first
love, they couldn't pretend

Often they wished, to turn back time, oh, for time to
have stood still!

Aye, to turn back time, but time goes on, it's nature's
will.

To return some day, they said they would, but I knew
— we never could.

Chapter 12

POLICE MOVE IN

Edmonton detectives Ian Shoaf and Jim Cessford flew to Southern Ontario in January 1988 — on the fifth anniversary of Tania's abduction.

They wanted to talk to Lorne Thomas, now a prime suspect. Thomas had moved back to Ontario in the spring of 1983, a few months after Tania vanished.

The officers wanted their man sober and so they knocked on his door at six in the morning. They were surprised to see Lorne suddenly open the door, as though he was expecting them.

Thomas was taken to a hotel room in Sarnia where the officers peppered him non-stop with questions — for 11 hours. That's not a typo. Eleven hours.

Police video-taped the interrogation. The recording is on file at the main police station in downtown Edmonton.

Because the Tania Murrell case remains open, all evidence — including that video — remains confidential. I've not been able to watch it.

According to Detective Shoaf, Thomas initially denied writing the poem ['Could Never Be'], but then owned up to it.

Thomas also downplayed his relationship with the Murrell family, claiming he barely knew them. He also said he'd forgotten their daughter's name.

Let that sink in.

However, when the detectives asked Thomas if he had any thoughts on who took Tania, his response was that only two people knew. "Me and God."

The detectives offered Lorne a charge of second degree murder [as opposed to 1st degree], plus therapy. Second degree usually means less prison time.

It was a compromise that officers felt would help everyone — especially with closure. The victim would also get a proper burial.

Thomas' response was: "Fuck you! You ain't got a body ..."

He was right. Police didn't have a body. For all they knew, Tania could have been living a good life, perhaps as a spoiled princess in the Middle East.

I was never able to reach Lorne to ask him about the lengthy interrogation. I flew to Toronto in 2015 after receiving a tip that Mr. Prime Suspect might be living on the street in the downtown area, but nothing came of it. Not a sign of him. No pun intended, but a bum lead.

In late 2018, I did meet with his relatives near Sarnia. They knew all about Lorne talking to two detectives in 1988 because Lorne had told them about it.

The family staunchly defended Lorne — especially his son, Brent Thomas.

Brent pointed out that his father met with the police officers *voluntarily* — and that he could've walked out at any time but chose not to. Again, we're talking 11 hours.

He described his father as a good man who stopped drinking when he started his family, and that was years ago.

Brent pointed out his father worked hard at an industrial job in Sarnia [Clysdale Heat Treating] — often in pain from a cancer he knew would kill him.

The son became agitated when I asked if Lorne had ever been charged with pedophilia, or suspected of it. His response was quick and stern. 'NO!!"

I raised some points with Brent — already covered in this chapter — about how Lorne told detectives that only two people knew what happened to Tania ['Me and God"] — and his father telling the officers, "Fuck you! You ain't got a body ..."

The son's take was that his dad was just "fucking with the cops." In other words, putting them on ...

It was the second time Lorne Thomas had been interrogated by Edmonton Police.

The first time was at the main police station, just days after Tania vanished. Thomas was given a lie detector — known in law enforcement circles as a 'truth verifier' — but that the results were inconclusive because Thomas had been drinking.

The man was never given a second polygraph. Don't ask me why.

Later on, reports began to pour in from the Murrells and their friends about Thomas' erratic behaviour.

Here's one account: While on an outing with the Murrells, Thomas reached over and turned off the ignition — while the vehicle, a station wagon, was still travelling.

Jack, following behind on his motorcycle, watched his car plow into the ditch. When he found out what caused the crash, he laid a beating on his drinking buddy.

Trailer Park Boys plus.

A biker named Melsi recalled a time when he and Lorne Thomas shared an apartment in Edmonton. They were sitting at the kitchen table, he says, drinking and playing cards when Lorne suddenly grabbed an empty beer bottle and — without provocation — smashed him in the face.

That's hardly proper etiquette when having a friendly game of cards with a biker.

Stunned, Melsi tumbled to the floor. But he didn't stay down long. He got up and pounded Lorne out.

It's touching moments like that we never get to see in those beer commercials.

The two men never shared accommodation again.

I asked Melsi if he had any thoughts on who might have taken Tania. He quickly replied, 'Lorne!' ... adding he always suspected the guy.

"Shit," I said, "did you ever mention that to the police or the Murrells?" "Nope," he said, "didn't want to get involved ..."

More *Trailer Park Boys* stuff.

Heather Hansen was one of the first to speak up. "Lorne always gave me the creeps," she says. "He could out-manipulate a manipulator."

She shared with Vivian her suspicions about the guy, but says nothing came of it. "The first time I told Viv that Lorne gave me the willies, she told me I was nuts and to have another beer."

In Heather's mind, Lorne Thomas will always be the prime suspect. The woman will go to her grave thinking he was responsible.

The babysitter, Brenda, described Lorne as very intelligent and somebody who read a lot. "He liked to write poems, putting his thoughts down on paper."

"But when he drank," she cautioned, "he couldn't re-member a bloody thing. He became polarized and passed out."

Another observation from the babysitter: it was hard to have eye contact with Lorne because his eyes darted all over the place. "He was nervous, jittery ... with his fin-gernails bitten."

"He seemed kind of mellow, not feminine, not queer," she said, "... not manly, but not a wimp."

Over coffee, Detective Shoaf revealed that a day or so before Tania disappeared, the Murrells were at a restaurant and Tania was acting up. The parents couldn't figure out what was bothering her.

Had the child been traumatized?

Police eventually shared with Vivian and Jack that Lorne Thomas — their drinking buddy — was a prime suspect.

It was now sinking in that one of their 'friends' could be responsible for such a heinous act. As Detective Shoaf put it, "They finally worked it out."

However, the couple still found it extremely difficult to believe that one of their friends would do such a thing.

When detectives first questioned the Murrells about Lorne Thomas, Vivian exclaimed, "Not him!! He's our friend!!"

On the 10th anniversary of Tania's abduction, I spoke with Vivian by phone. She'd settled down in Kelowna. Tania's mother sounded more focused ... and at peace. Somewhat.

It was clear Vivian had moved on ... but that her daughter was always in her thoughts.

And so was Lorne Thomas in her thoughts ...

All Vivian would say about their one-time drinking bud — in a full-out sob — was, "Do you know how I feel about that, Byron? It was me who brought him into our family ..."

Jack reacted differently. He phoned one time — I believe it was the only time Jack ever called — and he was looking for a number where he could reach Lorne, now living in Ontario. I passed on the phone number for Lorne's mother, Esther Thomas.

Jack was living out West and Lorne was thousands of miles away.

Tania's dad never did travel to Ontario to confront the prime suspect. Jack once told police that if he ever caught Lorne, they'd never find his body.

Jack eventually caught up with Lorne — by phone.

I discovered this when I met with Lorne's aging mother. It was the fall of 2018 and Esther, in her late 80s, was living on her own in Corunna, a small town near Sarnia.

Mrs. Thomas recalled her son getting a surprise phone call from Jack Murrell and that Jack had threatened to kill Lorne's daughter, Tina ...

Esther became visibly upset, asking if it was true that Jack Murrell would take her grand-daughter's life. "Unlikely," I said. "I don't believe Jack wanted to harm your granddaughter. He wanted to kill your son, Lorne."

Esther then broke into tears and walked away to grab some tissues. Her reaction was further proof of how far the ripples of Tania's disappearance had gone.

Jack never did find Lorne.

But cancer did.

In the summer of 2016, the prime suspect died on a cot in the living room of his home, a converted fire hall, surrounded by his family and a care-worker.

It was an overcast day with light rain falling when I located Lorne Thomas' small grave marker in a small cemetery in Courtright.

In January 1988, I had been aware that police were Ontario-bound to interview Lorne Thomas because Detective Shoaf had told me so.

Ian and I shared information, which began with me giving him the poem Thomas had written.

My take-it or leave-it advice to Ian was that while Lorne was a drunk, he wasn't stupid — and if he played chess with Lorne, he'd likely lose.

The comment wasn't meant to piss off Detective Shoaf, although it likely did. It was just an honest assessment; a heads-up.

The two detectives also went around to Thomas' old high school, went through some old reports and discovered Lorne Thomas had a high IQ, much higher than average.

Shoaf later shared that more than a dozen people — who knew both Lorne Thomas and the Murrells — felt that Thomas had taken Tania.

Put it another way, it wasn't exactly a big secret.

Terri, a friend of the Murrells, was another who suspected Lorne. She said he was often intoxicated, occasionally passed out, either on the couch or on the floor.

She thought that when Lorne drank he had a 'split personality.' "He'd sit at the table drinking — calm and collected — then fly into a rage. Next day, he was fine."

But in the end, all that meant little — now that Lorne Thomas is dead and not around to defend himself.

Yet, the man's behaviour remains a damning indictment. How is it that so many have similar suspicions and assessments?

Was Thomas really "fucking with the cops" ... or was he guarding a dark secret and taunting police? We may never know.

Edmonton Police point out that Thomas had no solid alibi the day Tania vanished. This neither hurt nor helped him.

In a wrecker's lot, officers located the sedan the prime suspect drove the day Tania was taken but they couldn't get any evidence from it because by then — more than four years on —- too much time had passed.

At the end of the day, police found themselves in a legal no man's land. They had some evidence — enough to lay a charge — but not enough to snag a conviction.

And so, Lorne Thomas was never charged.

All things considered, it's not difficult to see why detectives felt that Thomas was a prime suspect. Too many red flags.

The detectives' last words to Thomas were, "Don't hang yourself, you fucker, we want you alive ..."

Chapter 13

THE FAMILY VANISHES

It was September, 1987 when we got word that the Murrells — Vivian, Jack, John and Baby Elysia — had quietly slipped out of town. They'd relocated to the Okanagan Valley in South-Central British Columbia. Exactly where was anyone's guess.

My boss, Senior Editor Cam Ford, suggested I book a flight to B.C. and look for them. I said sure thing.

I focused on Kelowna, the largest city in the area. As soon as I arrived, I started moving from one noisy construction site to another. It seemed logical that Jack — a carpenter — would have found some work in construction.

But he hadn't. No one at any the construction sites I visited had even heard of Jack Murrell.

Was Jack now using a different name? And where was his wife and two children?

Finding the Murrells was like trying to find a needle in a haystack. The Okanagan is a big place and I ended up running here and there. Thank goodness my rental had unlimited mileage.

I then started hitting up the trailer parks. This also seemed logical given the Murrell's financial situation.

Pay dirt!! The manager of a sprawling complex on the edge of Kelowna revealed that the Murrells had stayed a while with one of his tenants ...

He referred me to Melsi — the same Melsi who'd been boinked in the head with a beer bottle courtesy of Lorne Thomas. Turns out, the biker was good friends with Jack and Vivian. No surprise there.

So I went around to see Melsi. His trailer had no steps and I had to reach up to rap on his door. The door opened ... and there stood Mr. Biker himself.

Melsi was a rough sort, but he was okay. He was certainly a tough bugger, dropping three feet to the ground and landing with a thud in the dirt — in his bare feet, no less — and not being fazed by it.

Oh. Melsi owned a big, noisy motorbike — and put it this way — it wasn't a shiny Gold Wing.

The man drew a map where I could find his buds. I followed his directions and drove perhaps ten miles north, way out of town in any case, stopping briefly at a store to pick up something. And no, it wasn't flowers or chocolates or a Harley magazine. It was something more practical.

It was pitch dark when I pulled up at a small cabin surrounded by trees and overlooking a lake. Before I knocked on the door, I stood quietly and listened for voices inside. When I heard Jack and Vivian talking, I knocked.

Jack opened the door. "Aw fuck!" he announced, turning back to break the news to his family. "They found us ..."

I wasn't welcomed — but my 12-pack of cold beer was greatly appreciated and that got me in the door. And for that idea, I have to thank Lorne Thomas ... he often pulled up at the Murrells' house with a case of beer.

I assured the Jack and Vivian I wouldn't reveal their location — but that some people back in Alberta wanted to know if those who had contributed to their charity had been ripped off.

Vivian did the talking — what's new — and just as well because Jack was hot under the collar after being 'discovered.' He stomped around the kitchen while I interviewed his wife at small table, all the while nursing our beer.

Not Jack. He was guzzling his beer.

The Murrells were now making their living by picking fruit in one of the many orchards in the Okanagan Valley.

Their lives had really been turned upside down. Within just a few years, Jack and Vivian had gone from well-paid jobs [bakery manager and construction] to seasonal work, picking fruit ... and living in a tiny cabin.

And it all began to change on January 20, 1983 ...

The explanation Vivian offered was that things got too heavy in Edmonton and her world was caving in. She said it had been well over four years since her daughter had vanished, and she couldn't go anywhere without people asking her about it.

The money from her charity, the Tania Murrell Missing Children's Society, was all accounted for, Vivian assured. "Everything's all here," she said, breaking away to point to some dirt-covered boxes on the balcony.

Vivian promised to get in touch with Alberta Consumer and Corporate Affairs and explain everything.

Was all the money accounted for, like she said? Or did money from her charity help pay off some family debts? It was impossible for me to tell. I was there to find the Murrells and interview them, not audit their books. I wasn't trained for that, and I hate numbers anyway.

According to Harold Baker at Alberta Consumer and Corporate Affairs, Vivian kept her word and phoned.

I can't say if the financial issues surrounding Vivian's charity were ever resolved. Baker didn't seem overly worried, if that meant anything.

Who knows? Perhaps a kind-hearted government bureaucrat sat back in his big leather chair, twirling a pencil and pondered ... what's really important here? Missing money — or a missing child? Let me see ...

Maybe the Alberta Government gave Jack and Vivian a break — the same way it gives multi-billion dollar breaks to oil and gas companies ... and a pat on the back to industrial polluters.

Please forgive the sarcasm.

We polished off half the beer that night, okay, maybe all of it ... and in the end, only Jack got blitzed — but he calmed down, the kids went to sleep and we parted on good terms.

It was the last time I saw Jack and Vivian.

Chapter 14

I t's my guess that **Tania Murrell** is deceased, her life snuffed out on the very day she was abducted. I also suspect her remains were buried — where, is anyone's guess.

Tania's disappearance may remain shrouded in mystery for decades, perhaps forever.

I believe in an Afterlife — and that Tania has now reunited with her parents and her brother, John — because they're all gone too.

Jack Murrell battled diabetes and had a leg removed before dying from kidney failure in British Columbia in 2005. Jack was only in his 40s.

Vivian Murrell died early as well. She hooked up with a new man and on New Year's Day, 2011, he returned from work to find his girlfriend lifeless on the couch.

Vivian had died from a brain aneurysm. She was 52.

The last time I had a good chat with Vivian was in January, 1993 — on the tenth anniversary of Tania's disappearance. It was an interview for *CBC Radio*.

Vivian shared some painful recollections of the day Tania left, some touching memories of her daughter, the controversy surrounding her charity, how her family was doing, the shame of knowing the prime suspect, her frustration with Edmonton Police ... and a message of appreciation to the people of Edmonton.

Tania's younger brother, **John Murrell**, was in and out of jail for much of his adult life. He was staying at a halfway house on Edmonton's south side when, in late January, 2015, he took his own life.

According to police sources, Tania's brother slipped a white electrical cord around his neck and hanged himself in a closet.

The troubled man was also doing street drugs. An autopsy showed John was using methadone, an opioid drug.

The young boy who had walked classmates home from elementary school became a drug addict with a lengthy criminal record. He died young. 37.

Family friend Heather Hansen wonders if John returning to Edmonton didn't open some old wounds. Tania and John were inseparable, she recalls. "When Tania went missing, John was scared shitless — and lost. The kid was devastated."

Elysia Murrell is the only surviving member of the family. She lives in Niagara Falls, Ontario.

According to published reports, Elysia, who was born after Tania disappeared, believes the sister she never knew is alive somewhere.

The prime suspect, **Lorne Douglas Thomas,** died from cancer in Courtright, Ontario in 2016.

He was cremated, "as per his wishes."

Think about this: If we could go back in time to the early 1980's and walk in the Murrell House — we'd hear rock music blaring and see Vivian tidying up in the kitchen ... buds Jack and Lorne in the living room smoking, drinking and bullshitting ... Tania and John in their bedroom playing ... and Harley the dog on the floor, curled up like a cinnamon bun, taking it all in.

They're all gone. Tania. John. Jack. Vivian. Lorne. Harley ...

Even the small bungalow is no more. It was demolished in late 2018.

I wonder if the current owners of the house [at **10426 - 145 Street**] know the sad story of the little girl who once lived at that address ...

Clairvoyant **Ralph Hurst** has crossed over as well. Cancer.

Story time: Whenever I round the corner at Jasper Avenue and 142 Street [in Edmonton], I often have the same flashback — a conversation Ralph and I had at that very same spot in the late 1980s.

I had mentioned to Ralph that there was a $25,000 reward ... and if his information on a prime suspect was spot on, he'd be entitled to the money, at least some of it.

But Ralph wanted none of it. Not a penny.

"Hell," I said, "then give it to Tania's parents ... they sure could use it." But Ralph disagreed. He felt Jack and Vivian had made poor choices that led to their daughter being abducted and murdered.

I never shared that with the Murrells.

Vera Stortz [Vivian's sister] is in Edmonton.

Heather Hansen, who lives in Leduc, south of Edmonton, still cries over Tania. And she'll likely cry when she reads this book because it too will open old wounds.

"When Tania went missing," she recalls with a sigh, "it was the hardest and saddest thing I had ever experienced ..."

Cam Ford — my boss when I worked for *CBC Radio*.

In the late 80s, Cam moved Down Under after his wife got a job teaching at the University of Melbourne.

After years of complaining about our *CBC* lawyers in Toronto, Cam went back to university ... and ... became a lawyer. How's that for Karma?

JT Lemiski is still in the news business and breaking stories. He's a newsreader/reporter at *CFCW Radio*.

Warren Michaels — the *CBC-TV* reporter who joined me at the back door of the Murrell house one cold winter day — left MotherCorp and ended up doing communications work for Cold-FX.

Warren is retired and living in Edmonton. I run into him now and then at Costco.

Ruth Anderson retired from the news business. Ruth had been news director of *CTV News* in Barrie, Ontario. She had a distinguished career in broadcast journalism.

Peter Hutchinson became station manager at *CBC Radio* in Victoria, British Columbia. The former *BBC* reporter is long retired.

Peter Pocklington is out of hockey. He's also out of a California jail where he spent time for fraud. Here's 'Peter Puck' with two students from my journalism class ...

PI Bruce Dunne is retired and living in British Columbia. Bruce went on to do some outstanding investigative work on the Colin Thatcher murder case.

Celine Stevenson, who chummed with John Murrell in elementary school, lives in Evansburg, Alberta.

Detective Jim Cessford left Edmonton Police and became Chief of Police in Delta, British Columbia. He retired in 2014. I never met the man and can't say what he's up to now.

Detective Ian Shoaf retired from the Edmonton Police after battling some serious medical issues.

For a while, Ian worked law enforcement for the Alberta Government. Last I heard, he was driving a transport truck.

We still get together for coffee and discuss the Tania Murrell case. I guess that's pretty well all we ever talk about.

Before we shook hands and said good-bye outside a Tim Horton's, Ian remarked that Tania may forever be a missing persons file.

We both hope he's wrong.

The **Author** is semi-retired and living in Edmonton.

He has no plans to retire ... that's for old folk. He plans to stay in the news business until he too checks out.

His first interview on The Other Side will be with ... you know who.

The first question will be, "Tania, what happened? ..." And when he meets Jack and Vivian — as I'm sure he will — with Jack hollering, "He found us!" — he'll apologize for not solving this puzzle.

It's a promise he made a long time ago.

Author

B yron Christopher has been an investigative reporter for nearly 40 years. Much of his career focused on true crime, such as the Tania Murrell story.

Byron has worked with most major radio and television networks — in both Canada and the United States — in addition to news agencies such as *Canadian Press* and *Associated Press.*

He has worked both mainstream and alternative media.

Byron has won two national awards for investigative journalism. He has also lectured at high schools and universities in Canada and Europe.

Google 'Byron Christopher wiki' for a write-up about his reporting career.

If you feel you'd like to share some leads or theories on what may have happened to Tania, please feel free to do that. Here's how to connect:

byronchristopher@yahoo.ca
Phone: 780.716.4693

Manufactured by Amazon.ca
Bolton, ON

12354721R00053